TWENTY

P9-APT-010

MONSTER MACHINES

Written by Mike Hirst
Illustrated by Laszlo Veres

Copyright © 2005 Top That! Publishing plc.

Tangerine Press

an imprint of
SCHOLASTIC
www.scholastic.com

Scholastic and Tangerine Press and associated logos are trademarks of Scholastic Inc.
Published by Tangerine Press, an imprint of Scholastic Inc., 557 Broadway, New York, NY 10012
10 9 8 7 6 5 4 3 2 1
0-439-78529-4
Printed and bound in China

24 SEVEN Contents

Monster Machines	3
Big Rigs	4
Long Haul	6
Monster Trucks for Fun	8
Many Loads	10
Big Buses	12
Large-scale Luxury	14
Jumbo Jets	16
Monsters in the Sky	18
Space Giants	20
Monster Earth Movers	22
Building Highways	24
Colossal Cranes	26
Digging Deep	28
Mining Monsters	30
Leviathan Liners	32
Shipping Giants	34
Monster Firefighters	36
On the Farm	38
Colossal Roller Coasters	40
Rail	42
Clearing Up	44
Logging	46
Glossary	48

Modern life would be impossible without machines. You probably use hundreds of them everyday: from simple tools such as scissors, computers and TV sets to elevators, automobiles, and airplanes.

Farther and Faster

Monster machines are the giants of today's world. With their help, we can build higher, dig deeper, and travel farther and faster than ever before. They transport people and goods, and they make our lives easier by doing difficult jobs for us.

Monster Spotting

Some of the machines in this book are very rare—you would be lucky to see any of the world's largest submarines as they are usually underwater, far out at sea. Other monsters are more common. Keep your eyes open, and you are bound to spot some amazing giant machines at work on a highway, farm, or construction site near you.

The Space Shuttle, Endeavour lifting off.

A monster fork-lift truck lifting logs.

When it comes to transporting huge, heavy loads, big rigs are the monster machines for the job. The strength of the big rig comes from its powerful engine, located inside the tractor at the front. The goods to be carried, called the payload, are transported on the trailer.

The Freightliner Coronado

The Coronado is manufactured by Freightliner. It is one of the company's most modern big trucks. Under the hood, the Coronado has a class 8 diesel engine. Most trucks run on diesel fuel, rather than gasoline. The most powerful engines have up to 525 horsepower. (By comparison, the engine of a typical family-sized automobile has only about 130 horsepower.)

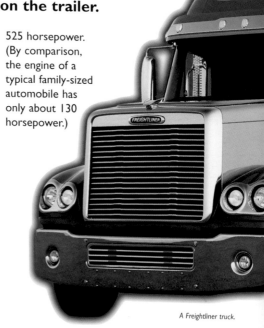

A Freightliner truck.

Fuel and Radiator

The radiator measures a massive 1,500 sq in. (11.6 sq. m) It has to be that large to cool the enormous engine. The Coronado has two fuel tanks. Each one can hold 140 gallons (529.9 l) (That's ten times larger than the single fuel tank of a medium-sized automobile.)

Exhaust Fumes

Two exhaust pipes carry exhaust fumes from the engine. They are cab-mounted, which means they run up either side of the cab like chimneys, so that the fumes do not come out at ground level.

A close-up of the "fifth wheel" disc connection.

The Fifth Wheel

The tractor and trailer of a big rig are connected by a "fifth wheel." This is not like the other wheels of the truck at all, but is a large disc fixed flat at the back of the tractor. This disc slots into a connector on the trailer. It keeps the tractor and trailer joined together, but allows the trailer to swing behind the tractor as the truck goes around corners. The tractor and trailer are also connected by lines that take electricity to the trailer to make its brakes work.

Long-haul trucks travel huge distances. As the drivers may be away from home for several days at a time, these trucks have specially-designed cabs so that the driver can sleep and rest in comfort, as well as travel safely.

A Home Away from Home

Inside a long-haul cab you can find the same kind of equipment as a top-grade motorhome: storage shelves and cupboards; a high-tech sound system; power outlets and a TV antenna; even a refrigerator. Some cabs have two bunks, so that a team of two drivers both have a bed when they make long journeys together.

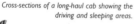
Cross-sections of a long-haul cab showing the driving and sleeping areas.

T-Class Cabs

Scania T-Class cabs are built for trips lasting thousands of miles. They are made out of a tough steel cage, enclosed by steel panels. Computer-controlled robots weld the steel of the cab together so that it will not break if there is an accident. Technicians have tested these structures, and the roof does not crumble even if a $1\frac{1}{2}$-ton weight is dropped on it from a height of 10 ft (3 m).

Road Trains

A really powerful tractor can pull more than one trailer. A vehicle with two or more trailers is called a "road train." The longest single road train was 4,053 ft (1235.3 m) long, with a single tractor pulling 87 trailers at Mungindi New South Wales, Australia in 2003.

Some Monster Trucks are made just for fun. With a fairly standard four-wheel drive pick-up truck body on top of four enormous wheels, these are amazing vehicles. You can see them at stunt events and Monster Truck races across North America.

Bigfoot

The Bigfoot series is the prototype for all Monster Trucks, and one of the fleet is still the world's largest Monster Truck. The first Bigfoot was built in the 1970s, when a St. Louis construction worker started to make changes to his pick-up truck, so he could drive it off-road.

A Bigfoot Monster Truck.

Massive tires are needed for Bigfoot's wheels.

Record Breaker

Today, the record-breaking *Bigfoot 5* stands more than 15 ft (4.5 m) off the ground, mainly because of its towering 10 ft (3 m) high wheels. It has Firestone Tundra tires and weighs more than 2,400 lbs (1,088 kg). Like all Bigfoot trucks, the body itself is not really that large. It is simply a customized Ford F-series pick-up truck.

Jumping

Jumping is another exciting stunt. The truck drives as fast as it can up a ramp and flies off of the top. The enormous tires help to cushion the landing. However, the highest ever Monster Truck ramp jump had a bumpy landing. *Bigfoot 14* took off from a massive 24 ft (7.3 m) high ramp, but when it hit the ground, the force was so great that one of the front wheels snapped off its axle.

A Bigfoot Monster Truck performs a jump.

Car Crushing

The classic Monster Truck stunt is driving over the top of a row of junk automobiles. The stunt is called "car crushing" and it is possible because the huge wheels of the Monster Truck do not get stuck as they drive across the automobile roofs.

A Bigfoot Monster Truck crushing cars.

Trucks are customized to carry many different types of load. The design of the trailer or goods compartment depends on what cargo the truck is meant to transport.

Flat-Beds

A flat-bed trailer has no walls or roof. Chains and ropes hold the payload in place. A bulkhead, or metal wall at the front of the flatbed, stops anything from sliding forward and hitting the cab.

A flat-bed truck hauling a locomotive.

A moving truck holds furniture.

Moving Trucks

A high, dry van carrier is good for transporting large objects. It makes an ideal removal truck, with room for big pieces of furniture and packing crates. A low floor makes it easier to load or unload.

Live Loads

Livestock trucks need openings for fresh air and light, so that the animals can travel in comfort.

This tanker is carrying petrol – a very hazardous load.

Dangerous Loads

Tankers are designed with curved sides to carry liquids, and sometimes also pressurized gas or chemicals. A number code on the tank tells everyone what is inside. A diamond-shaped warning-sign shows clearly if a tanker is carrying a dangerous load—such as poisonous liquid or gas that catches fire easily.

Auto Transporters

Automobile transporters are usually articulated double- or triple-deckers. The top deck can be raised or lowered to let automobiles drive on.

Staying Cool

Refrigerated trucks have a cooled container to keep food fresh.

Trucks are fine for carrying goods, but how do you transport large numbers of people on the roads in one vehicle? Buses and coaches are the answer.

Omnibus

Our word "bus" comes from the Latin word "omnibus," which means "for everybody." The first omnibus was a horse-drawn vehicle, which could seat around 30 or 40 people. It does not seem too big to us today, but it must have looked huge when it first appeared on the streets of modern cities like New York in the late 1800s. (Some early omnibuses ran on tracks, like a tramway, which created a smoother ride.)

A horse-drawn omnibus.

Jumbocruiser

Probably the biggest bus of all time was the Neoplan Jumbocruiser. Only about ten of these monster coaches were ever built.

'Round the Bend

The Jumbocruiser is a double-decker. It is also articulated, which means it is built in two parts with a concertina bend in the middle, so it can go around curves easily, even though it is more than 60 ft (18.2 m) long. The Jumbocruiser's engine is located near the middle of the coach.

Articulated Buses

Although the double-decker Jumbocruiser is very rare, you can see single-decker articulated buses in many towns and cities across North America. With its sleek design, the NABI 60-BRT is one of the most modern. At 60 ft (18.2 m) in length, it seats 60 passengers and has three sets of doors.

An articulated bus.

A monster coach.

The Rolling Hotel

For a monster coach experience today, you could try the "Rotel." It's a coach and hotel all in one, devised by a German tour company. The largest coach can seat as many as 40 people, who sleep "on board" in bedrooms in an attached trailer. An exciting "all-terrain" bus, it can transport 20 people on expeditions to remote parts of the world such as deserts and mountain regions, where it can drive on dirt roads and tracks.

With enough money, you can cruise the highways in large-scale luxury.

Stretch Luxury

Stretch limousines are extra-long automobiles with many extra comforts. They are ideal for special occasions, like a wedding or a movie premier. They are called stretch limousines because they really do look as though they have been stretched, with a much longer space between the front and back wheels. The extra length makes a much larger area for carrying passengers—the back of the automobile usually looks like a smart lounge.

Record Breaker

The longest stretch limousine ever is 100 ft (30.4 m) from end to end. It was customized by Jay Ohrberg of Burbank, California, and needs 26 wheels to carry the monster body. It even has its own swimming pool!

A black stretch limousine.

Airstream Comfort

Motorhomes and trailers are a great way of traveling long distances without giving up the comforts of home. Airstream classic trailers have been touring America's highways for more than 70 years. They hitch to an automobile or pick-up with a trailer bar. The trailer's beautiful curved body reduces the air resistance, so the vehicle towing the trailer uses 20 percent less fuel. (That's why the trailers are named "Airstream.")

An Airstream trailer.

The Skydeck

Motorhomes have the same facilities, but in a rigid truck structure —with the living area behind the driver's cab. The Airstream Skydeck is a true luxury giant. At 39 ft (11.8 m) in length, it has a Freightliner truck chassis. Stairs inside the motorhome lead up to a sundeck on the roof where there are couches, tables and lounge chairs.

An example of a luxury motorhome.

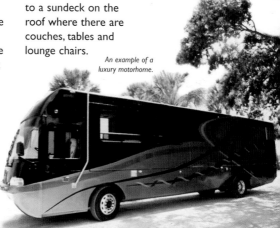

The jumbo revolution began in 1970, when the first Boeing 747 entered service with Pan Am. For more than 35 years, the 747 series jets were the world's largest passenger airplanes. Today, however, these jumbos have a rival—the superjumbo Airbus 380.

An Airbus A380 aircraft.

Airbus Innovations

Launched in 2005, the Airbus 380 is the largest airplane in production. It was developed as a joint project of companies in four European countries: the UK, France, Germany and Spain. In spite of its size, the designers have tried to build an environmentally-friendly aircraft, with good fuel consumption, and quieter engines.

Record Breaker

The Airbus 380 is 239 ft (72.8 m) long—that's about two-thirds the length of an American football field. The wingspan is even greater, at 261 ft (79.5 m). More impressive still is its height: 79 ft (24.0 m), or taller than a seven-story building. Although it is usually expected to carry about 555 people, the airplane is designed to have lots of space for passengers to move around on two large decks, with features like a lounge and sleeping areas. However, if more seats are installed, the Airbus 380 can transport as many as **840 people** at one time.

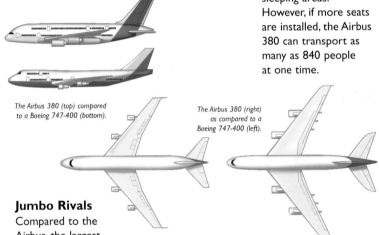

The Airbus 380 (top) compared to a Boeing 747-400 (bottom).

The Airbus 380 (right) as compared to a Boeing 747-400 (left).

Jumbo Rivals

Compared to the Airbus, the largest Boeing jet, the 747-400, is almost as long at 231 ft (70.4 m), but it has a shorter upper deck and stands at 63 ft (19.2 m) tall. The Boeing 747-400 can take a maximum of 524 passengers, but is usually configured to hold around 416 people.

Boeing vs. Airbus

But is bigger really better? The Airbus 380 has an impressive range, of more than 6,900 miles (11,104 km), yet some critics say that it is not as useful as the Boeing 747. The Airbus 380 can only land at the world's largest airports, with wide, long runways. It is really a "hub-to-hub" aircraft. The largest Boeing 747s, on the other hand, can land in more places, and already serves more than 210 airports worldwide.

Jumbo passenger jets are the most common airborne giants, but there are other, even bigger machines in the sky. Cargo planes are built to carry huge loads. Airships are even bigger, though a very rare sight in the skies nowadays.

Cargo Twins

Many jumbo passenger jets also have a cargo plane "twin." The Airbus 380, for instance, has a three-deck cargo model, the A380F, which has a shorter range (just 4,800 miles (7,724.4 km), but can carry a massive 335,000 lbs (150.1 kg) payload.

The Airbus A380F.

An Antonov An-225 carrying a space shuttle.

Record Breakers

The largest cargo plane, the An-225 Mriya, was built in the former Soviet Union by the Antonov Design Bureau. It has a payload of 551,150 lbs (250,001.6 kg)—that's the same weight as 246 average-sized elephants.

Dream Airplane

Mriya means "dream" in Ukrainian, and only one original version of the airplane was built. It was designed with a single, vast cargo hold, to transport a space shuttle, and entered service in 1989. Unfortunately, when the Soviet Union split up in the early 1990s, Russia and the Ukraine abandoned their Buran space shuttle program, and the An-225 went out of use. However, its unique ability to transport very large objects brought it back into operation in 2001.

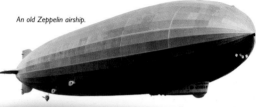

An old Zeppelin airship.

ZEPPELIN NT

A Zeppelin NT airship.

Airships

Airships have fairly small cabins, so they can not carry really heavy loads or many passengers. Yet the huge, helium-filled envelopes which lift them off the ground make them the largest objects in the sky made by humans.

German Giants

The biggest airships were the *Hindenburg* and the *Graf Zeppelin II*, both 803 ft (244.7 m) long, and built in Germany in the 1920s. Seven of these airships standing in a line would stretch for a mile (1.6 km). Today, however, the largest working airship is the Zeppelin NT. It only carries 14 passengers, though its 246 ft (74.9 m) envelope is still longer than the largest airplane fuselage.

19

Some of the largest engines in the world are needed to power space vehicles. It takes a huge amount of energy to escape the pull of the Earth's gravity. To travel into outer space, a vehicle must travel at 24,900 mph (40,071.5 km/h)—that's more than 15 times faster than a supersonic airplane.

Space Shuttle

The space shuttle is the first vehicle that can travel into space and return to Earth at the end of a mission. Before the space shuttle was invented, astronauts went to space in rockets, but most of the rocket was abandoned in space. The astronauts returned to Earth inside a tiny module.

Liquid Fuel

Three engines are at the back of the shuttle. They use liquid fuel, stored in a huge tank as big as a large swimming pool which is fastened to outside of the shuttle.

Launch

On its launch pad, the space shuttle stands higher than a 15-story building. It uses five engines to take off.

A Voyager launch, August 1977.

Booster Engines

Two more rocket engines are fastened to the sides of the spacecraft. They give the shuttle the extra boost it needs to travel into space. These rockets burn solid fuel. When the shuttle is 28 miles (45 km) high, the rocket boosters run out of fuel. They fall away and parachute back to Earth.

Rocket Giants

The world's biggest ever rocket was the Saturn V (left), developed in the 1960s to take astronauts to the moon. Standing a massive 363 ft (110.4 m) high, it launched the Apollo spacecraft, positioned at the rocket's nose. Unlike the space shuttle, each Saturn V rocket could be used for just one space mission.

In Space

Once the shuttle reaches space, it does not need power. The liquid fuel tank is empty, so it is jettisoned and burns up as it re-enters Earth's atmosphere. Now, smaller engines steer the shuttle, and position it when it is ready to return to Earth.

Shifting dirt, rocks and rubble is a job for true monster machines. These giants prepare the ground before construction begins on major new highways and buildings.

Bulldozers

A bulldozer is designed to have massive pushing power. With its large, wide blade attached to the front, it shoves huge loads of soil or debris along the ground ahead.

A massive bulldozer.

Record Breaker

The world's biggest bulldozer is the record-breaking Superdozer D575A-3, manufactured by the Japanese corporation Komatsu. It can push a load of more than 485,000 lbs (219,996 kg). Its giant blade, 24 ft (7.3 m) wide and almost 11 ft (3.3 m) tall, would dwarf any pick-up truck that gets in its way. To see over the top of the blade, the driver must sit in a cab 16 ft (4.8 m) high.

Excavators

Excavators have a strong lever arm to dig the ground. At one end of the arm is a "bucket" with jagged teeth for scooping up dirt. The other end of the arm is mounted on a large, rotating platform. The cab also swivels around, and the excavator can reach out in any direction.

An excavator.

Caterpillar Drive

Two driving wheels, connected to the engine, are raised at the front of the vehicle. Spikes around the rims of the driving wheels grip the caterpillar tracks firmly and make them go around. The caterpillar tracks are steered by idler wheels, usually mounted at the back of the vehicle, and raised off the ground like the driving wheels.

Caterpillar Tracks

Most excavators have crawler or caterpillar tracks, instead of ordinary wheels. The tracks are good at gripping slippery ground, but they also stop the heavy machine from sinking into soft earth. Caterpillar tracks spread the weight of a machine over a much wider area than ordinary wheels.

Caterpillar tracks.

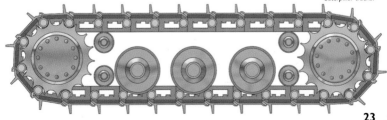

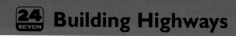

Modern highway construction calls for a variety of heavy duty machines, each doing its own specialized job.

Rough Preparations

Excavators and bulldozers prepare the ground roughly at first. Next, a scraper may be used to cut a path for the road to follow.

Scrapers

The scraper has a large, earth-carrying hopper, which can be lifted or lowered on hydraulic arms. At the front of a hopper is a sharp blade. If the hopper is lowered, the blade cuts into the earth as the scraper moves along, and pushes the waste earth up into the hopper. When the hopper is full, the scraper carries it away and dumps it at a place where it is needed to build up a bank.

A scraper.

Graders

If the ground is still rough, another machine called a grader comes along and smoothes the surface with a large blade. Then a compacter passes over the surface. It sieves a layer of small stones and crushed rock onto the road, and then drives backward and forward to squash this base layer down with a heavy vibrating roller.

A paver.

Pavers

Most roads have a top layer made of asphalt: a mixture of black, sticky oil, and sand or gravel. A machine called a paver mixes the asphalt and heats it up to make it runny. The paver drives across the road surface and spreads the hot asphalt over the road. When it cools, the asphalt dries and turns hard.

Compactors

Finally, another compactor rolls across the top layer of asphalt as it is drying. The heavy rollers make the road surface really smooth.

A compactor.

25

Cranes are the tallest machines in the construction industry. Reaching high into the sky, they lift huge, heavy loads from one place to another. You are most likely to see them on building sites, or at dockyards where they lift crates and containers on and off of ships.

Strong Weight-Lifters

The German manufacturer Liebherr produces the HC series of cranes. Some of these machines have towers standing 360 ft (109.7 m) tall. The crane's lifting arm is called the jib, and the strongest HC class can pick up weights of 176,000 lbs (79.8 kg)—that's as heavy as 176,000 bags of sugar.

Cranes are very useful when building tall blocks of flats.

Luff Cranes

A luff crane is especially handy where space is tight. As well as swinging in a circle, the jib of a luff crane will also lift to point upward, so that the crane can turn right around in a narrow, enclosed space. The Liebherr 800 HC-L lifts heavy-duty equipment to more than 320 ft (97.5 m), but turns in a circle that is only 52 ft (15.8 m) across.

A luff crane.

Colossal Cranes

Mobile Cranes

Because cranes are so tall, it's usually a long and difficult task to dismantle a crane from one site to move it to another. However, the monster Liebherr LG 1750 is a fully mobile crane, with a retractable tower and jib which fold down flat at the end of one job ready to drive to a new location.

A Liebherr LG 1750.

Supporting the Load

The LG-1750 is mounted on a massive chassis with 16 wheels mounted on eight axles. The large number of wheels make it very stable on the ground. The crane also has four extremely rigid, folding arms, which can be spread around the chassis once it is in place. The arms make a star-like pattern, and give the crane base even more stability. Once the base is absolutely firm, the crane tower and jib can be extended. This crane can lift a weighty 700 tons and has a top lifting height of 625 ft (190.5 m). The jib can reach out a distance of more than 325 ft (99 m).

27

Look out for diggers on construction sites, where they make deep holes for the foundations of buildings. Mines and quarries are also great places to see huge excavating machines.

Backhoe Loader

A backhoe loader is a classic digging machine, rather like an excavator, but with huge wheels so it is more mobile. The backhoe is a digging tool with sharp teeth, fixed on the end of a long arm (or dipper) at the back of the machine. It works rather like a spade, and the largest backhoes can reach to a depth of 17 ft (5.1 m). At the front of the machine is a large bucket to carry the earth dug out by the backhoe. Some buckets can hold four tons of earth.

A backhoe loader.

Hydraulics

The backhoe dipper is moved by a system called hydraulics. Each section of the dipper is connected to a piston that sits inside a tube, or cylinder. Each cylinder is filled with thin oil.

Moving the Pistons

The engine presses air against the oil, which flows into the cylinder and pushes against the piston head so that the piston moves forward. To make the piston move the other way, the engine pumps more oil into opposite end of the cylinder behind the piston head, which pushes it backward. As the piston slides forward and backward, it moves the parts of the machine.

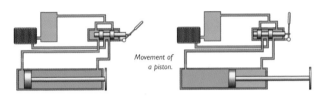

Movement of a piston.

Drag-Lines

A drag-line excavator is a really huge digging machine, used mostly in mines and quarries. It usually stays in one place for a long time, and can be moved only using a system of rollers, but it can lift huge amounts of earth— as much as 400 tons of material.

A drag-line excavator.

Excavating a Load

A drag-line excavator uses a system of cables and pulleys to scrape up earth. The drag-line bucket is held between several strong cables, attached to the top and bottom of a tall crane. When the lower cables are pulled, they drag the bucket along the ground, and it digs the top layer of earth as it goes. Then the crane lifts up the bucket and swings it around. When some of the cables are slackened, the excavator bucket dumps its load.

Mines and quarries are home to some giant vehicles. The harsh working environment, filled with dust, rubble and loose rocks, means that these machines must be extra-tough as well as extra-large.

Dump Trucks

Dump trucks carry rocks, stones or other construction materials such as gravel. The payload goes into a big, open box behind the cab. To unload the box, the whole back section of the truck lifts upward on two mechanical arms, and the goods being carried are tipped out onto the ground behind.

A Terex Titan.

Payload Box

The payload box is shaped like a "V" so that it gets deeper toward the front. If you look at a cross-section of a dump truck, you can see that this shape means that more weight rests in the middle of the truck. With the heaviest weight at its center of gravity, the truck is very stable and difficult to tip over as it moves around the uneven ground of a mine or quarry.

Tunnel Boring

One of the hardest mining jobs is digging a long tunnel underground. A special tunnel boring machine can cut a tunnel shape into rock or soil without disturbing the ground above.

Shield and Blade

The tunnel boring machine is a huge cylinder, called a shield, with a large, sharp cutting blade at the front. The blade spins round and chips away at the rock or soil, while the shield supports the empty space just behind the blade.

A massive tunnel-boring machine.

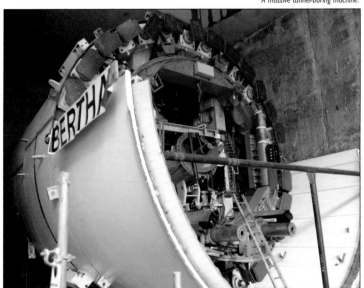

Making a Tunnel

Other equipment works alongside the tunnel-boring machine. The cut rock or soil has to be carried away, often on a conveyor belt. At first, jacks support the tunnel roof and sides, but as the tunnel-boring machine moves forward, rail tracks may be put down so trucks can bring in concrete sections to line the inside walls.

Passenger ships are the way to transport the most people at one time. Moving at around 30 mph (48.2 km/h), liners are much slower than jumbo jets, but they can move thousands of people together in comfort.

Queen Mary 2—
the world's largest
passenger ship.

Queen Mary 2

The world's largest passenger ship is the Cunard Company's liner, Queen Mary 2. She made her maiden voyage in 2004 and carries a staggering 2,620 passengers, served by 1,253 crew —that's more people than many small towns. Standing as tall as a 20-story apartment building, and longer than three football fields laid end-to-end, Queen Mary 2 is a true monster machine. She has 13 decks, 10 restaurants, five swimming pools and her own playing field.

Sailing Ships

The largest ever sailing ship was France II. She had five masts, and all her sails put together covered an area more than 60,000 sq ft (5,574 sq m). Sadly, this majestic giant only sailed for ten years before she was wrecked in the Pacific Ocean in 1922.

Riverboats

Even riverboats may be extra large. The *American Queen* cruises along the Mississippi River, carrying 450 passengers in grand style. Spread across the six decks are sleeping cabins and public rooms such as the Grand Saloon, parlor and a theater. The *American Queen* is powered by a giant paddle wheel, 28 ft (8.5 m) across. Although she was launched in 1995, the American Queen is modeled on the great paddle steamers that first appeared on the Mississippi in 1811.

A paddlewheeler river boat—Mark Twain—on the Mississippi.

Automobile Ferries

Huge automobile ferries are a common sight in the British Isles. They are designed so that passengers can travel to Ireland or mainland Europe in their own automobiles. A huge door at the front or the back of the ferry allows vehicles to drive into the hold. The lower decks of the ship are like a big, floating parking lot.

A passenger car ferry.

Tankers, container vessels and aircraft carriers are the very biggest ships to be found on oceans around the globe.

Aircraft Carriers

The US Navy's Nimitz-class aircraft carriers are the largest military ships in the world. Measuring 1,092 ft (332.8 m) from bows (or front) to stern (or back), they are not quite as long as some other boats, but they are very wide. At 252 ft (76.8 m) across, they can support a 4 $\frac{1}{2}$ - acre flight deck, with space for 85 aircraft on board. They also carry a huge crew, with 3,200 sailors needed to operate the ship, plus another 2,480 air force personnel for the aircraft.

The nuclear-powered aircraft carrier, USS Abraham Lincoln.

Launching from a Nimitz

Ten Nimitz-class aircraft carriers have been built. They are vitally important for the US military as they allow air-force jets to operate far away from home. In battle conditions, the Nimitz can launch one aircraft every 20 seconds.

Typhoon Submarines

The largest submarines are Russia's Typhoon class. First produced in 1981, they are 574 ft (174.9 m) long. Each submarine has two powerful nuclear reactors on board, which provide enough power to keep the vessel operating underwater for months at a time.

The USS Salt Lake City submarine cruises at full power on the surface of the ocean.

Record-Breaking Cargo Carrier

The world's largest cargo ship, the oil tanker, *Jahre Viking,* is also a monster survivor. She is 1,504 ft (321.2 m) long and 226 ft (68.8 m) wide. She was almost totally wrecked during the Iran-Iraq War of 1987-8, but was later restored and relaunched.

A cargo container ship.

Container Ships

Most dry cargo is transported inside metal boxes called containers, loaded onto huge container ships. The *Shenzen,* built in South Korea, can carry more than 8,000 20 ft (6 m) long containers. In weight, she transports more than 98,000 tons of cargo. Even more amazing is the size of the ship's crew. The *Shenzen* is almost totally computer operated, so she only has 19 people on board.

Fire trucks are large and fast. They have to travel quickly to fires and other dangerous situations, but they also need enough space to carry a lot of different equipment.

Fire Truck Equipment

A fire truck is built to do three important jobs with one single vehicle. First, it carries the firefighting team to emergencies. Second, it is a tool box, packed with specialized equipment for the firefighters. Last, it contains a pump that sucks water from a fire hydrant to sprays it on the fire. Most fire trucks also carry tanks containing foam and some water in case none is available at the scene of the fire.

Airport Firefighters

You will find the very biggest fire-fighting machines at airports, where they stand by in case of airplane emergencies. The *Rosenbauer Panther* is a massive machine. The largest models have eight huge wheels and a water tank containing 2,750 gallons (10,409.9 l) of water. Another two tanks each contain 1,600 lb (725.7 kg) of fire-extinguishing foam. In spite of its huge size, it still has a top speed of 85 mph (136.7 km/h).

Aerial Ladders

Fires are especially dangerous in high buildings, and the HD-75 has an aerial ladder, which reaches 75 ft (22.8 m) into the air. The ladder rests flat on the roof of the truck as it moves along. It is joined to the truck by a large hinge. At the scene of the fire, the hinge moves to point the ladder upward, and interlocking sections of the ladder slide out to make it longer.

A huge firetruck with an aerial ladder.

Pumping Water

The Amercian LaFrance HD-75 is a standard, all-round fire truck, with a tough, stainless steel body. The crew cab has seating for a full team of firefighters. The fire hose is up to 1,000 ft (304 m) in length, and the pump delivers 2,000 gallons (7570.6 l) of water per minute at full flow. The on-board water tank contains 500 gallons (1892.6 l).

Monster machines are an important part of life on modern-day farms. In minutes they carry out tasks that used to take days of hard work by farm hands.

Combines

The combine harvester is one of the largest farming machines. When crops such as wheat or rye are ready, a food grain harvester does several jobs at the same time.

Through the Harvester

A reel or platform sweeps the plants neatly beneath the front of the harvester, where a blade cuts the stalks. The cut stalks are then transferred up into the body of the machine where a thresher separates out the heads of grain. The grain is then sieved and passed up to the grain hopper, while the threshed stalks are churned out of the machine, where they can be bundled up into bales of straw.

A combine harvester.

Awesome Augers

Combines use augers to lift grain and move it around inside the machine. An auger is a huge screw inside a tube. As it twists, it lifts the loose grains and moves them along the shaft of the screw. Augers were first used thousands of years ago in ancient Greece.

An auger.

A tractor.

Farm Tractors

Like combines, tractors do many different farm jobs. They have powerful engines and big wheels, so they can pull all kinds of tools across rough, muddy fields.

Towering above the world's biggest amusement parks, colossal roller coasters deliver monster thrills! Riders sit in small, wheeled passenger cars that speed around the tracks of these terrifying machines.

What Goes Up...

A roller coaster works by hauling the cars up a steep slope to a high point near the beginning of the ride. An engine inside a starting station powers a moving chain that runs alongside the tracks of the big slope. At the start of the ride, the cars connect to the chain, and the chain then drags the line of cars up to the highest point of the roller coaster.

...Must Come Down

At the top, the cars unhook from the chain and start to roll downhill. Now, the force of gravity does the rest. The cars go faster and faster down the hill, until they have built up enough speed to carry them right up to the top of the next slope, and so on. Gradually, the "hills" become lower, until the cars reach the starting point again.

A massive roller coaster.

Colossal Roller Coasters

Feeling Heavy

The movement of the roller coaster gives each rider two very strange feelings. As the riders speed downhill, they feel heavier and heavier, because the forward movement of the cars combines with the force of gravity, which pulls us all down toward the ground.

Roller coaster riders.

Record-breaking Roller Coasters

The world's tallest roller coaster is *Superman the Escape* in California. It is 415 ft (126.4 m) high, although the track does not go around in a complete circuit—when they have gone down the slope, the passenger cars are pulled backward to the start of the ride. The highest, traditional circuit roller coaster is the *Fujiyama* in Japan. The first drop of the ride is 230 ft (70.1 m) —that is about the same height as a 20-story building.

Feeling Light

However, as the train races uphill, the riders feel lighter and lighter, because the forward movement of the cars cancels out much of the downward pull of gravity.

Railroad engines are the original monster machines. They were carrying huge loads right across North America long before trucks and automobiles were invented.

Steam Power

The first railroad trains had coal-powered steam engines. A fire inside the locomotive heated water to make steam, which pushed pistons and made the wheels turn. The largest steam locomotives are the 4-8-8-4 Big Boys, built by the Amercian Locomotive Company in 1941-44. Each engine is 130 ft (39.6 m) long, and weighs 500 tons.

A steam locomotive.

An Amtrak locomotove.

Diesel Power

Today, most railroad engines use diesel fuel or are powered by electricity taken from overhead cables. The largest diesel-fuel locomotive ever built was the Union Pacific DDA40X "Centennial." It was almost 100 ft (30.4 m) long and had a fuel tank that contained 8,000 gallons (30,282.4 l) of diesel fuel.

Electric Locomotive

The biggest ever electric locomotive was built by General Electric in 1948. Only three of these locomotives were constructed, and they all worked pulling freight trains on the South Shore Line. They were just over 88 ft (26.8 m) long.

An electric locomotive.

Denver Ski Train

Several railroad companies claim to have the longest trains. In the U.S. the longest regular passenger service is the Denver ski train, which carries tourists more than 50 miles (80 km) from Denver to the ski resort of Winter Park.

Monster Goods Train

The longest train ever was another iron ore transporter in western Australia. It had seven engines, 682 trucks and 5,648 wheels, all measuring more than $4\frac{1}{2}$ miles (7.2 km) long. The train weighed a mammoth 98,150 tons.

A coal-carrying freight train.

Utility trucks are an essential part of modern life. They keep our towns and cities running smoothly by taking away refuse and doing the kind of clearing and cleaning jobs that are just too big for people without a monster machine.

Garbage Trucks

Garbage trucks have to be reliable, heavy-duty vehicles, that operate steadily for hours every day. Today's trucks usually have a large, enclosed body for carrying trash. It is made out of reinforced steel.

Big trucks take away our garbage.

Collecting the Trash

Many trucks have an opening at the back. Trash is tipped into a large hopper, and from there is shoved forward by steel blades into the body of the truck. The packing mechanism is important, because the truck can carry more trash if it is crushed up really tightly. To unload the refuse, hydraulic arms lift up the body of the truck.

Trucks that crush garbage can carry more trash.

Side Loaders

More and more places are now recycling certain types of refuse, and a new-style truck can collect different types of trash for recycling at the same time. The Heil Formula 7000 has a side-loading automatic arm that lifts trash cans and unloads the contents into one of two separate compartments in the body, depending on whether the trash can be recycled or not.

Snow Clearing

In some regions, clearing away snow is just as important as clearing away trash. Snow plows are ideal for making a single path through deep snow, so that other vehicles can pass behind. The plow works by pushing snow away to either side of a large blade.

Massive machines clear snow from the roads.

Snow Blowers

A snow blower, on the other hand, clears a path through snow by sucking it up into the machine and then throwing it out again somewhere else through a chute. Snow blowers are good for clearing large areas of snow, because they can load snow onto a truck which then dumps it at a distance from the area being cleared. Snow blowers are often used to clear airport runways or sports arenas.

Lumberjacks use powerful, robust machines to help them cut down trees and transport timber.

Feller Bunchers

Feller buncher vehicles look quite like tractors with big wheels and heavy-duty tires. However, the two front wheels are fixed to an axle which is separate from the engine and back part of the vehicle. The front axle moves independently with its own articulated body section. At the front of this articulated section is a powerful high-speed saw and guiding claws.

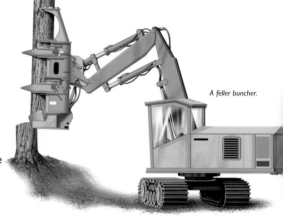

A feller buncher.

The feller's guiding claws hold the tree while it is being cut.

Preparing the Timber

The feller puts the guiding claws around a tree trunk and the saw cuts it down in just a few seconds. Then the guiding claws tighten around the tree trunk. They twist around and lay the trunk flat on the ground.

46

Harvesters

A tree harvester is even larger and can do more jobs. It looks rather like an excavator, with a long, hydraulic arm. However, the end of the arm has a large grapple claw as well as a high-speed saw. Once the harvester saws have cut down a tree, the grapple picks it up and slides it along through the claws, to strip the tree trunk of its branches. The harvester saw then cuts the tree into the right length of logs before piling them up.

A tree harvester.

Skidders

Skidders are vehicles that pull tree trunks around the forest once they have been cut down. They usually have a grapple on the end of a thick metal cable, attached to a winch that pulls trees toward the skidder as it winds in. However, some skidders have a grapple attached to the end of a long, hydraulic arm. Skidders gather trees ready for loading onto trucks for further transport.

Articulated
If an object is articulated, it has two separate sections connected by a hinge or joint.

Atoms
Everything in the universe is made up out of very tiny particles called atoms. Atoms are too small for us to see with ordinary microscopes and it takes millions of atoms to make even small objects.

Axle
A rod or pole with a wheel at each end. The axle spins round as the wheels turn.

Chassis
The flat metal frame of a vehicle, that supports the wheel axles, engine and bodywork.

Concertina Bend
A hinge made by folds in a piece of material or plastic.

Customized
A customized vehicle has been changed to make it different from any other vehicle of the same model.

Fire Hydrant
A water pipe and faucet, connected to the main water supply in the street.

Four-Wheel Drive
In a four wheel drive vehicle, all four wheels are connected directly to the engine that turns them.

Fuselage
The main body of an airplane.

Gravity
The force that pulls everything toward the earth and which makes objects feel heavy.

Helium
A gas that is lighter than air. It is used to fill balloons and airships to lift them off the ground.

Hopper
A container that is narrower at the bottom and wider at the top.

Horsepower
The strength of an engine is measured in horsepower. One horsepower equals roughly the pulling strength of one horse.

Hydraulic
In a hydraulic machine the parts are moved by pressing a liquid against them. The liquid is called hydraulic fluid.

Jet
A jet engine sucks in air at the front and pushes it out at the back with great force.

Nuclear Reactor
A very powerful engine, that works by changing how the atoms in the nuclear fuel are joined to one another.

Piston
A metal rod that slides up and down a cylinder, pushing and pulling other moving parts of a machine.

Rocket
The simplest but most powerful type of engine. The rocket is pushed along by the force of the gas made when the rocket fuel burns.

Thresher
A machine that hits, or threshes, plants such as corn, to separate the edible grains from the rest of the plant.

Tractor
A vehicle that pulls a trailer or other piece of equipment with wheels.

Wingspan
The distance across an airplane from the tip of one wing to the tip of the opposite wing.

Acknowledgements

Key: Top - t; middle - m; bottom - b; left - l; right - r; NPL - Naturepl.com; NSP - Natural Science Photos.

2: NASA. 3: Lester Leftowitz/Corbis. 4-5: Freightliner LLC. 8: Bigfoot 4x4 Inc. 9: (t)Bigfoor 4x4 Inc; (b)Duomo/Corbis. 10: Alvey and Towers. 11: (t)Christine Osbourne/Corbis; (b)Freightliner LLC. 12: Topham Picture Point. 13: (t)Alvey and Towers; (b)Freightliner LLC. 14: Rick Gomez/Corbis. 14: Topham Picture Library. 16: Rex Features. 18: Aviation Picture Library. 19: Rex Features. 20-21: NASA. 22: Rex Features. 23-27: Alvey and Towers. 31-33: Topham Picture Point. 34: Corbis. 35: (t)Steve kaufman/Corbis; (b)Topham Picture Point. 36-37: Freightliner LLC. 40-41: Topham Picture Point. 42: (t)Topham Picture Point; (b)Ed Koshi/Corbis. 43: (t)Flat Earth; (b)Topham Picture Point. 44: (t)Alvey and Towers. 45-47: Alvey and Towers.